What Is a PREPOSITION?

by Sheri Doyle

Consulting Editor: Gail Saunders-Smith, PhD

CAPSTONE PRESS
a capstone imprint

Pebble Plus is published by Capstone Press,
1710 Roe Crest Drive, North Mankato, Minnesota 56003.
www.capstonepub.com

Copyright © 2013 by Capstone Press, a Capstone imprint. All rights reserved. No part of this publication may be reproduced in whole or in part, or stored in a retrieval system, or transmitted in any form or by any means, electronic, mechanical, photocopying, recording, or otherwise, without written permission of the publisher.

Library of Congress Cataloging-in-Publication Data
Doyle, Sheri.
  What is a preposition? / by Sheri Doyle.
     p. cm. — (Pebble plus. Parts of speech.)
  Includes index.
  Summary: "Full-color photographs and simple text provide a brief introduction to prepositions as parts of speech"—Provided by publisher.
  ISBN 978-1-62065-131-5 (library binding)
  ISBN 978-1-4765-1731-5 (eBook PDF)
1. English language—Prepositions—Juvenile literature. 2. English language—Parts of speech—Juvenile literature. 3. English language—Grammar—Juvenile literature. I. Title.

PE1335.D69 2013
   425'.7—dc23   2012031640

Editorial Credits
Jill Kalz, editor; Heidi Thompson, designer; Marcie Spence, media researcher; Laura Manthe, production specialist

Photo Credits
Alamy Images: Wim Wiskerke, 13; Getty Images, Inc.: Don Johnston, 11, Liz Banfield, 17; iStockphotos: jlmatt, cover (boy), VikramRaghuvanshi, cover (girl); Shutterstock: Anna Jurkovska, 9, Arie v.d. Wolde, 5, Artistic Endeavor, cover (cookies), Denis Babenko, 15, Foonia, 8, iker canikligil, cover (milk), Inna G, 7, kwest, 21, michaeljung, cover (boy sitting), Stephanie Frey, 19, Xavier gallego morel, cover (girl in box)

Note to Parents and Teachers

The Parts of Speech set supports English language arts standards related to grammar. This book describes and illustrates prepositions. The images support early readers in understanding the text. The repetition of words and phrases helps early readers learn new words. This book also introduces early readers to subject-specific vocabulary words, which are defined in the Glossary section. Early readers may need assistance to read some words and to use the Table of Contents, Glossary, Read More, Internet Sites, and Index sections of the book.

Printed in the United States of America in North Mankato, Minnesota.
092012   006933CGS13

Table of Contents

What It Does 4
Where? 8
When? 12
More Prepositions 14

Glossary 22
Read More 23
Internet Sites 23
Index 24

What It Does

Where is the frog? *On* the lily pad. A preposition is one part of speech. It ties words together to show how they are related.

A prepositional phrase is a group of words. It begins with a preposition. It ends with a noun or pronoun.

The young ducks swim **behind** their mother.

The young ducks swim **behind** her.

Where?

A preposition often shows where an object is. These words are common prepositions: in, out, on, off, by, behind, under.

in the box

on the phone

by the papers

A preposition may show where objects are moving. Objects may move "up" or "down," "to" or "from."

The skunks run across the grass.

They run toward their mother.

When?

A preposition often shows when something happens. The movie may start "before" lunch, "after" lunch, or "during" lunch.

The kids play outside during the rain shower.

More Prepositions

Prepositions can help answer these questions:

Which dog digs?

How does it dig?

Why does it dig?

The dog <u>with</u> brown fur digs.

The dog digs <u>with</u> its paws.

The dog digs <u>for</u> its bone.

Prepositions point to more facts about an object.

Who is this girl?

What does she want to be?

Selena is one of my sisters.

She dreams of becoming a doctor.

A preposition may be found anywhere in a sentence. It may be the first word, the last word, or somewhere in between.

After it rains, the trail is muddy.

Leave your boots on.

Prepositions are right *in* front *of* you! They help you understand the connections *between* words *in* a sentence.

Glossary

connection—the joining of two or more objects

noun—a word that names a person, place, or object

object—anything that can be seen or touched; a thing

prepositional phrase—a phrase that begins with a preposition and ends with a noun or pronoun

pronoun—a word that takes the place of a noun

related—to be tied to one another in some way

Read More

Heinrichs, Ann. *Prepositions.* Mankato, Minn.: The Child's World, 2011.

Loewen, Nancy. *If You Were a Preposition.* Word Fun. Minneapolis: Picture Window Books, 2007.

Walton, Rick. *Around the House the Fox Chased the Mouse: An Adventure in Prepositions.* Layton, Utah: Gibbs Smith, 2011.

Internet Sites

FactHound offers a safe, fun way to find Internet sites related to this book. All of the sites on FactHound have been researched by our staff.

Here's all you do:

Visit www.facthound.com

Type in this code: 9781620651315

Check out projects, games and lots more at
www.capstonekids.com

Index

common prepositions, 8
finding prepositions, 18
prepositional phrases, 6
sentences, 18, 20
showing
    how, 14
    movement, 10
    what, 16
    when, 12
    where, 4, 8, 10
    which, 14
    who, 16
    why, 14

Word Count: 175
Grade: 1
Early-Intervention Level: 23